From Vision to Action

From Vision to Action

Tricia Neill

Alpha International
London

ISBN 10: 1 90407 487 1
ISBN 13: 978 190407 487 8

Published by Alpha International
Holy Trinity Brompton, Brompton Road, London SW7 1JA
Email publications@alpha.org

Design by Karen Sawrey

Foreword

For all of us who have been involved with Holy Trinity Brompton, Tricia Neill is an institution. Her professionalism, clear-sightedness and common sense pervade every aspect of the church's life.

For many years we had a dream that the way we ran things in Christian circles would rival the best of what we saw elsewhere. But we did not know how to do it. Now we do. You find a Tricia – and stand back!

She came to us, of course, with considerable experience of top class management, latterly with Rupert Murdoch's News International group where she ran their exhibition and conference division.

I remember well her arrival on our staff in 1994, soon after completing an Alpha course at the church. Within a very short time, meetings were being organised – each with a clear purpose and direction. Notes were being made of decisions which were then acted upon.

Gradually Tricia built up a culture of professionalism across the whole staff which I was privileged simply to watch and wonder at.

Amid all this activity, Tricia's grace, kindness and tact has been at the centre of it all. Her sheer sensitivity to those around her is abundant. I cannot think of anybody who has felt anything other than built up by what she has to say – even difficult things.

Those of us who have worked at Holy Trinity have been convinced that – 'Every church needs a Tricia.' But I'm afraid HTB hope to hang on to her for some time yet!

In the meantime, with the help of this little booklet, we can all now share her wisdom and expertise.

Sandy Millar

ASSISTANT BISHOP, DIOCESE OF LONDON
VICAR OF HOLY TRINITY BROMPTON 1985-2005

Contents

Why this booklet?

This booklet is primarily concerned with the 'ins and outs' of church management. It is for leaders of churches of all sizes, who are looking for effective ways to carry out whatever vision God has given them – leaders of churches who want to 'move their church forward'.

I have been asked time and time again how we have worked through growth here at HTB and this booklet helps to address these questions.

> *Why shouldn't the church work more professionally and better than any good secular organisation?*
>
> Sandy Millar

A part of the HTB vision is to share what we have been given by God with other churches. 'Giving it away' is one of our driving philosophies. I hope that through this booklet we are 'giving away' some of the knowledge we have gained and some of the lessons we have learned along the way. It represents a collection of tried and tested methods that we have been using and improving upon for more than twelve years.

It has been an enormous privilege to be involved in the growth of the Alpha course. I never fail to be excited by the stories of lives changing and churches growing the world over as a result. Here at Holy Trinity Brompton, we experienced this growth when Alpha became central to all that we did. As new people joined our church, we addressed the way we ran things.

Sandy Millar, former vicar of HTB, asked me early on in my time here: 'Why shouldn't the church work more professionally and better than any good secular organisation?' When training churches to run the Alpha course, we encourage them to treat their guests better than any secular course would treat them. Sandy was instrumental in setting this high standard for the running of the church as well.

Nicky Gumbel – pioneer of the Alpha course and now vicar of HTB – has remarked that there are three types of people: those who make things happen, those who watch things happen and those who haven't a clue what's happening. While I suspect many of us would like to be in the first category, I think we all too often fall into the last.

At HTB we have learned many lessons. I am not writing this to say that we know it all, because we certainly do not, and we learn every day from the experience of other churches. I hope you can relate to some of what follows and apply it to your own churches to enable you to get where you want to go.

I recognise that for many our situation at HTB – even twelve years ago when we had 27 staff – may not seem relevant. I know that many churches have no paid staff at all. Nevertheless, we use many of the same approaches for working with volunteers and staff and set the same standards. In addition, many people who have worked at HTB have found that the techniques they have learned have proved to be very useful when they subsequently moved on to churches of different sizes. As I have developed this booklet, people involved with churches, large, medium and small, have reviewed it. I have been most grateful for their enthusiasm and input.

Finally, it is important to state early on that everything we try to do at HTB is undergirded with prayer. We know that without prayer the approaches discussed here would not amount to much.

It has been a great privilege to work with Sandy Millar and Nicky

Gumbel and I am grateful for the opportunities they have given me, which form the basis of this booklet.

I would like to thank Jamie McLean and Jo Rice for the fun of working with them and for their assistance in writing this. I am also grateful to Mark Elsdon-Dew, Alpha International staff and all those who have read the manuscript, for their wisdom and input.

We hope you will find the ideas helpful and wish you every success in moving your God-given vision forward.

Tricia Neill

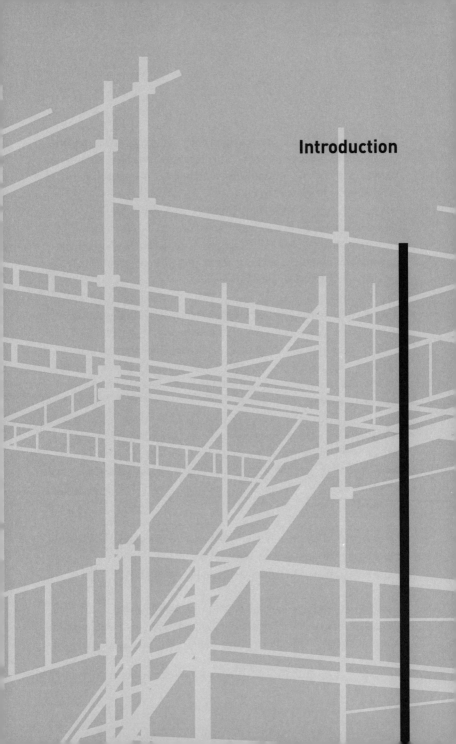

Introduction

I was brought up in Northumberland and I had a very happy, normal childhood. As a family we went to the local Presbyterian church every Sunday, and my early years revolved around Sunday school, youth club, tennis and swimming.

All I ever wanted to do was teach, so as soon as I left school I went off to train as a teacher. I was terribly excited about leaving home, and from that moment I never went to church again. I just didn't see the relevance of Christianity for my life.

After qualifying as a teacher, I went to teach at a primary school in Newcastle on a desperately poor housing estate. I hated it. I couldn't cope with the children at the school. They were so badly behaved. I did have a good social life and knew lots of people so life wasn't all bad, but still I always felt there was more to life than I was experiencing.

In my third year of teaching, I saw a job advertised in the Sunday Times. Shell, the oil company, had schools for children of their workforce all around the world – and they wanted teachers. I applied, and after about six months of interviewing I was offered a job in the Sultanate of Oman.

I'd never heard of Oman but in 1978 I went to live there. I knew within two hours of my arrival that I completely loved it. I loved the country, I loved the school, I loved the children, I loved the life.

I stayed in the Middle East for seven years. Within a year, I was made deputy headmistress of the school. I enjoyed every moment of my job and the lifestyle it afforded – boats, helicopters, parties, drinking and a whirling social life.

Eventually my contract ran out with Shell and I had to leave. I came back to London in about 1985 and decided that I didn't want to teach anymore. I was keen to try something new.

Within a week of being in London, a friend I'd met in the Middle East phoned me up and said, 'Trish, our company is desperate for help. Can you come out?' The company was called World Trade Promotions, and the job was helping to organise and set up exhibitions all around the world.

Towards the end of my first week there, the Managing Director asked me to stay. The exhibitions were in Hong Kong, Chicago, Brussels and other major cities. All of them were abroad and I loved travelling, so I said yes. It was a tremendous training ground for me.

Five years later, in 1990, I was approached by News International, owned by Rupert Murdoch, to set up an exhibition company for them. They asked me to spearhead a new company, which would put on consumer exhibitions marketed through their British newspapers (which at the time included The Sun, News of the World, The Times, The Sunday Times and Today).

I was really excited about it because it was a new company and I love starting up new things. We began recruiting lots of people, and soon we were doing events all over the UK. I was involved in quite a fast executive lifestyle by then. I worked hard and I played hard too.

One of the highlights of my week after moving to London was that I joined a tennis club in Wimbledon (the Wimbledon Club, opposite the All England Club), and used to play every Saturday. I made many good friends at the tennis club. Two of the girls there went to church, and one day they invited me to an Alpha supper party at their church.

They told me there would be lots of nice people there and it would be great fun, and I liked them so I thought I'd try it. I'm usually game for something new.

When I went to the Alpha supper – at a church I didn't know at the time called Holy Trinity Brompton – I didn't really enjoy it. The food and the company was good but the after-dinner talk by a speaker called Nicky Gumbel was just too much for me. I didn't like it at all.

'You ought to go to this Alpha course. You'll meet some nice people there'

When Jean, one of the friends who had invited me, asked how it had gone and whether I might consider going on an Alpha course, I said, 'Jean, I'm seriously not interested and I'd be grateful if you'd never mention it to me ever again.'

And to my horror I added, 'And if you want I'll come with you and keep you company.'

Tricia Neill

About nine months later I was chatting to a neighbour who lived opposite me. As we were speaking she told me, with tears in her eyes, that her husband had been having an affair with his secretary for some time. She said, 'I don't know how I'm going to get through this. All my friends are very superficial and just party people.' I felt so sad for her and didn't know how to help.

Then I heard myself say to her, 'You ought to go to this Alpha course. You'll meet some nice people there' And to my horror I added, 'And if you want I'll come with you and keep you company.'

She said, 'I'd like to go'. And I thought, 'Help! I'm going on the Alpha course!' So I went to Alpha in January 1993.

When I arrived for the first week of the course I was shocked.
Here were all these nice, normal people discussing if God existed.
But what if he did? What difference was it going to make? On the way
home I felt so unsettled by it all that I said to my neighbour I had to
stop for a whisky – so we pulled in to a pub.

Despite this inauspicious start I gradually found that my attitude
began to change. I began to go for myself. I wasn't going just to keep
my friend company any more, and I was intrigued. I began to join in
the group discussion, and soon realised that I was looking forward to
each week.

On the Wednesday morning after the Alpha weekend, I was sitting
at my dining room table. I had started reading the Bible, and was
reading about the cost of being a disciple when I thought, 'I want to
be a Christian. I would give up everything and anything for that.'
So I prayed and told God that I was sorry and I wanted a new start.

That morning – it was in February 1993 – I gave my life to Jesus.
I was so excited. It was like I was in love for the first time – an
extraordinary feeling. My priorities began to change - my lifestyle
that had previously been so important no longer seemed to matter.

When the course was over I was invited to
help on the next course, and the next one.
I also joined a prayer group. One day, some
months later, I got back to my office at
News International and there were three
telephone messages on my desk.

One said, 'Please call Nicky
Gumbel urgently.'

I suddenly felt an overwhelming desire that everyone there should have the opportunity to attend an Alpha course.

The next one said, 'Please ring Jeremy Jennings' *[the Financial Director of Holy Trinity Brompton]*.

And the third said, 'Please ring Judy Cahusac *[HTB's Alpha course administrator]* urgently.'

So I thought, 'Well, something is up.'

I rang Nicky and he very sweetly asked me if I would be prepared to leave my job and come to HTB to work with him. He didn't quite know what my job would be, but could I finish my job today and start on the following Monday. That's typical of Nicky.

I laughed and said, 'I don't think so, Nicky.' And that was it.
Or so I thought.

The following Tuesday I went to my little prayer group and they asked, 'How's your week been?' I said, 'You won't believe this...'

And I roared with laughter and said, 'Nicky Gumbel asked if I would come and work with him at Holy Trinity Brompton.'

And they said, 'Well, what did you say?'

And I said, 'Well, I said "no" of course.'

And they said, 'Well, don't you think you should pray about it?'

I was completely shocked. As a new Christian I hadn't thought of that. So after that I started praying.

That weekend, at a friend's very traditional wedding, I looked around at the lovely group of people attending and was moved by the thought that this occasion might be the only opportunity they had to hear the gospel. I was sitting in the back row, and as I watched all of these people sitting in front of me I just started crying. I suddenly felt an overwhelming desire that everyone there should have the opportunity to attend an Alpha course.

While I was still genuinely struggling with the idea of saying 'yes' to the job, I began to feel I just couldn't say 'no.'

About two weeks before I finally accepted, I was offered the position of Director of News International Exhibitions. It was the post I had wanted – everything I had been working for, with a huge pay increase and so on. But when I was offered it, I just thought, 'So what?' It didn't mean anything to me. When I finally rang Nicky to accept HTB's offer, I knew I had made the right choice.

On my first day working at Holy Trinity Brompton, in April 1994, I drove in at about 8:30am and opened the boot of my car. I got my stuff out. I looked around, and I couldn't find anybody. I could not find a single person. Eventually I came across a man with a hammer in his hand. I said, 'I wonder if you could help me? My name's Tricia and I'm just starting today.' He beamed at that and said, 'Oh! I'm just off to build you an office.'

I was terribly upset because they'd known I was coming for three months. But when I came, I had no office, no desk, no phone. I had nothing. I remember feeling very sorry for myself and thinking, 'I've given up so much – and this is what I've come to.'

We definitely reaped positive results from applying business principles in a Christian way.

Later on I remember thinking, 'No other staff member's ever going to have that happen to them when they arrive so long as I am here.'

As I went around to meet the staff (there were about 27 at the time), everyone was very helpful and enthusiastic but there was very little structure to what they were doing. There were no job specifications. Nobody knew who was reporting to whom. In a sense they were not making the most of the advantages they had, being what was – even then – one of the biggest and most well-known churches in the UK.

During my first year at HTB, I was working mostly on helping to support the growth of Alpha outside of HTB. Alpha was exploding, and many churches were interested in running it. However, we found that after a year all we had done was react to the demand. We had not actually planned the way forward in a structured, systematic way.

I recall saying to Nicky that I had never previously approached my work in this way – merely reacting to circumstances, rather than planning where we were trying to get to. During that first year I used to feel as if I was trapped on a conveyor belt, and whilst all this was happening I remember being asked if I could manage with only a part-time assistant. My answer was firmly in the negative. The perception at first was that I did not need much help. There was a lack of understanding that the right administrative support could make our ministry so much more effective.

God has blessed us enormously over these twelve years. We now have 161 staff working on Alpha International and HTB, located on two separate sites. When I arrived there were 200 Alpha courses, and now there are over 31,000 in 165 countries. Eight million people have attended an Alpha course. We have opened thirty-five Alpha offices around the world, and officially translated Alpha into sixty-three languages. The rate of growth was astounding, and in 2001 the decision was taken to set up Alpha International as a charity, separate from HTB. It was a very, very exciting time.

After about three years at HTB, we could see we were attaining the professional standards and structures for Alpha that we desired. Sandy also passionately wanted these things for HTB as the parish church – a natural consequence of Alpha being at the very heart of the church. We set about incorporating the ideas, professionalism and processes of Alpha into the running of HTB itself. At that time Sandy created a leadership team of himself, Nicky and I over both Alpha and HTB, so that we were responsible for all activities in both these areas. Each of the three of us had a clearly defined role – Sandy as the senior church leader responsible for the vision, Nicky as the practitioner, and myself as the implementer. This model worked very well, as there was one person on the team whose job it was to make it all happen.

We definitely reaped positive results from applying business principles in a Christian way, and during these last twelve years I have had the privilege of seeing six new church plants go from HTB, and seeing Alpha run with more than 1000 people involved; I have watched the growth of pastorate groups to more than 78, and seen the expansion of Sunday services to five. So I have to say from that first, bleak, Monday morning, life has certainly not been dull.

Casting the vision

Articulate your vision

Our vision statement at HTB is 'the re-evangelisation of the world
and the transformation of society.' You probably already have a
sense of what God wants to do through the ministry of your church,
or maybe there is simply an inner longing for change as you have
seen the impact of Alpha within your parish. The steps we at HTB
took to develop our vision have changed over the years, as we
ourselves have grown.

Set the baseline

When we first embarked on the systematic process of applying
business principles to the running of HTB, we looked at and
addressed what we believed God was calling us to do. We asked
ourselves what we thought our future should look like, and what
the vision for our church was.

We then looked at our current situation. We looked at what we were
achieving and what we were not. We noted where we were, and
where we wanted to be. We looked at specific areas like the number
of services, the number in the congregation and the profile of the
parish. That became the baseline for any comparison we were
working towards. For example, in a particular year, we decided we
wanted to see ten new pastorates[1] and twenty new volunteers to run
the children's work.

Each year when we report at the Annual General Meeting, or in our
Annual Report, we can chart our growth and see how far we have
come. We also review on a regular basis where we think we are

going. The review process is covered further in the next chapter.

Invest your energy in the vision

Once we knew the direction we were going in, we had to stay focused on what our vision and our values were. It was necessary to clarify our message, and in everything we did we needed continually to ask ourselves: 'Does this fit in with the aims and objectives of the vision that God has for us?'

Does this fit in with the aims and objectives of the vision that God has for us?

At one time a member of our staff, Emmy Wilson, was getting confused about what commitments to take on in her role, as churches were inviting her to speak on many different topics. For me it was simple, because I used to say to her, 'What are we trying to do? Where are we trying to get to?' Emmy's role was heading up the prison work, which we were very keen to see grow. I encouraged her to ask herself: 'Does that task move the vision forward or not? Does it distract you?' Of course, sometimes the Spirit will speak to us and release us, and we have to be free to do that. But on the whole, following the vision is the first priority.

So we would only undertake a project if it would move the vision forward. We have had many opportunities over the years to participate in other areas, but we have had to stay focused on what we believe is our specific calling.

Share the vision

In order for the vision to take root, it had to be shared with key people in the church, and the congregation as a whole. I remember in my first week on staff, I received a little bit of a difficult phone call from the accounts department on how much the development of Alpha outside Holy Trinity was costing the church. I remember being really shocked, and saying to Sandy and Nicky, 'You know, I'm not sure whether everybody shares the same vision. If this is what God is doing, I'm not sure that everybody, both on the staff and in the congregation, is on the same page we're on.' We didn't sit down and think through every possible channel of communication to impart and reinforce the message, but I did notice that Sandy, as the church leader, started speaking about Alpha and his vision for the church all the time. He was leading from the front and using every opportunity – the PCC, sermons, everything he did – to talk about what he felt God was doing. The more people understood and felt part of the vision, the more enthusiastic and committed they became.

> *The more people understood and felt part of the vision, the more enthusiastic and committed they became.*

It is important to recognise that you do not have to do it all on your own – even if you appear to be alone in your church. In our situation, Sandy Millar identified those in the congregation and among the church leadership who were also longing for growth and change. As a leader, you need to identify key people and put them around you – as staff, leaders, or other people in the congregation – to help you realise your vision.

We have needed to build up a team both within the church, and also from outside – a network of other, like-minded churches. At our conferences we encourage people to come as part of a team, and we then set up a time during the conference for churches from the same geographical area to meet up and get to know one another. This allows friendships and mutual support to develop.

It is really helpful, when you are struggling, to be able to talk to someone who understands your situation and is working towards similar goals. Similarly, you can be a great encouragement to others. All the leaders of HTB church plants (known as the Home Focus Churches) get together three or four times a year to meet and encourage one another.

No church's vision, however well thought through, will be realised without the commitment of the community who can make it happen. As Sandy used to say:

> 'Put the sign on the bus. What I simply mean is tell people as soon you can where you are going. Then they don't have to speculate. If you go out into the high street you will see a number of buses. They have numbers and stops. You can decide whether to get on. As soon as I could I said to them here at Holy Trinity Brompton, 'We are moving in the direction of the New Testament Church. It'll take time; we might go to Birmingham via Calcutta and Sydney, LA and Brighton, but it's to Birmingham that we are going, that is the direction.'

One church leader tells of how he lost a church plant because he did not repeat the vision enough to people he thought knew it already. In the end they left, and the plant died. Tell people where you are going. Expect to repeat yourself over and over again as you communicate your plans and priorities.

What follows is a structure that might help you to think through how to communicate your vision.

Most clergy overestimate what can be achieved in one year and underestimate what can be achieved in five.

John Wimber

Documenting your vision

There are a variety of tools which help to keep us on course and to communicate the vision effectively. These will form the basis for all your communication, whether written or verbal. For example:

The vision statement
This is a brief statement, only a few sentences, that summarises who you are and what you are hoping to achieve by carrying out the mission of your church.

The five-year plan
The five-year plan is the main vision document. It gives a long range view of where the church is heading, and where it will be within five years. John Wimber used to say: 'Most clergy overestimate what can be achieved in one year, and underestimate what can be achieved in five.'

The one-year plan
This is the action plan for the coming year, and the budget flows out of this document.

Quantifying the goals
Quantifying the goals within these action plans enables us to be more specific when communicating the vision. It helps to form images in the minds of people. For example, how many small groups would we like to see on Alpha? How many children attend our children's groups on a Sunday?

Who needs to experience the vision?

Once you have formulated and documented the vision, there are a number of different groups that need to hear about it. For example, at HTB we would communicate with the:

- *Church committee – (eg the PCC)*
- *Leaders (pastorate leaders, worship leaders, Alpha group leaders, children and youth leaders, etc)*
- *Staff*
- *Congregation*
- *Broader church community.*

Defining these groups is a key part in ensuring that the vision is shared appropriately.

What are the best ways to communicate to the different groupings within your church?

For each grouping, decide on the best means of communication. For example, when we moved to five services on a Sunday, we chose to hold a special meeting so that we could explain things fully and take questions straight away. When we are encouraging everyone to go to Home Focus (our summer holiday as a church family), we make a big announcement at church, have an article in our church newspaper, and send letters out with a brochure inviting our congregation to attend.

Identifying and developing communication skills is central to making sure that more people understand and therefore take on the vision.

We have found that identifying and developing communication skills is central to making sure that more people understand and therefore take on the vision. Where expertise exists in writing or speaking within your congregation, use it to help you communicate the message. Similarly, where someone has a skill in photography, web design or desktop publishing, do not be afraid to ask for help.

As many people in the church come from different backgrounds, education and cultures, we have discovered that when we share common experiences with a particular group of people we find it much easier to communicate with them. We therefore set aside a significant amount of time in the church calendar for creating those 'common experiences' – opportunities to build the relationships that enable us to share the collective vision effectively. Some examples are discussed below.

Church leadership committee e.g. PCC or eldership
Your church committee meetings are a key time to pray about and build on the vision of the church, and to ensure that all the church's activity is supporting that vision. We meet once a month and begin with supper before the business part of the meeting, as a supportive church committee will be based on good relationships made during this informal time. At HTB the PCC have a 'Quiet Day' once a year, to set aside all the day-to-day business of the church and discuss and pray about the vision God has given them.

Leaders
Leaders' Weekend – At HTB we hold an annual Leaders' Weekend at a conference centre in the country. We invite all the leaders in the church – pastorate leaders, Alpha group leaders and so on – to go away for a weekend together. Over the course of the weekend Nicky presents what he believes God is calling the church to, and will then work with the leaders and hear from them what the issues are.

Vicarage suppers – Nicky regularly opens up his home to invite the leaders in the church to come for supper and get to know one another, and to discuss the vision together and the part they may play in it.

External conferences – Nicky will seek to take leaders with him when he attends a conference or meeting that he feels might influence the direction of the church. In this way it is not only Nicky who comes back keen to bring about new ideas or changes, but a whole group that understand the values, reasons and models he is hoping to implement. In addition, relationships are built up by attending the same event. When delegates return, there are more people able to spread the message.

Staff

Staff Day – We have a 'Staff Day' every year, during which we talk about the direction the church is taking, and what that will mean for the staff. We also enjoy a leisurely lunch, and have time to pray for one another.

Staff prayer meetings – We hold a full staff meeting once a week (see later for more detail). Each meeting is dedicated to worshipping God, restating the vision, and giving feedback on how we are seeing God fulfil that vision week by week.

Project meetings – These meetings involve different members of staff, and the purpose is to plan and track individual projects and create a common understanding of where we are all going. These are practical meetings that serve to establish what needs to be done to move a project forward. They also ensure that the team knows why we took on the project in the first place – how it fits into the vision. These regular meetings help build relationships within the team as it goes along. This is particularly important for volunteer teams, where these meetings might be the only opportunity people have to spend time with other members of their team.

Congregation

Restating the vision to your congregation is essential – they need to own it. Repetition is key. You can do this in many ways.

Vision Sunday – We have two 'Vision Sundays' each year, on the Sundays before Gift Days, in September and March. In the sermon we explicitly set out the vision of the church, and what support it will require from the congregation.

Annual report – To coincide with the first Vision Sunday of the year, we produce our annual report. This document includes reports from all the church ministries (and a good number of photographs) explaining what has been going on in the past year, as well as showing the congregation how all resources have been allocated. We distribute a copy to every member of the congregation during the Sunday services.

Other Sunday sermons – We regularly take the opportunity on a Sunday to explain how the Bible passage we are teaching on relates to our vision. We give examples of how we see the vision being fulfilled. We talk about Alpha a lot, and have testimonies and stories of the ways God is at work. These are a powerful way of re-illuminating the vision for the congregation.

Website – Our website clearly expresses the vision of the church, both explicitly, by stating the vision statement, and implicitly, by describing all the activities the church is involved with.

Church newsletter – Once a month we publish a church newsletter for the congregation. It includes plenty of photographs, and provides news about what is going on in the church, including weddings and events, and information on new initiatives. It is also a key opportunity to restate the vision, and to tell stories of God at work in the life of the church.

HTB News – Every Sunday we show a short video of what is happening in the next few weeks at HTB. Our vision is restated through the activities that happen week by week in the church.

Church Weekend/Holiday – Every summer HTB hosts a week's teaching holiday for the congregation at a holiday camp on the coast. This is an important time for refreshing, re-focusing, and building relationships within the church. It is also an important time in restating the vision of the church and, if necessary, changing direction. While we have found a week to be an advantageous length of time, many of our church plants hold great weekend events.

AGM or APCM – In the Anglican Communion every church holds an annual meeting known as the Annual Parochial Church Meeting (APCM). This is where the PCC (church council) is elected and we review the previous year's activity and outline the vision for the future. The HTB congregation is encouraged to attend this meeting, to ask questions about the vision of the church and to take part in electing representatives. If an annual meeting is not a standard feature of your church, we would encourage you to consider it, as a year is a good timeframe for marking progress.

Parish Day – Every summer we host a 'Parish Day'. It is an opportunity for the whole congregation to come together and share a common experience. There are picnics, a bouncy castle, games and music. We all just have fun together.

Broader church community

No doubt you are involved with ecumenical groups and secular community groups, and you will want to keep them informed of your church's vision.

Refining the vision

> *Any vision is dynamic.*
> *It moves and grows*
> *with the organisation.*

Any vision is dynamic. It moves and grows with the organisation. It is important for any organisation to review its vision regularly, and to make sure that its communications are consistent with that vision. How does today's work – a year down the line – compare with the baseline you established when you started the whole process with your parish review? How have you moved on?

Be prepared to change as you go

At HTB we have often struggled because everything outgrew the structures we put in place. So we have had to create a new structure. I have been at HTB for twelve years and I think in that time we have probably restructured three times. Each time we have gone back to the drawing board, armed with new knowledge and new ideas on our direction, and asked the question – 'How do we make sense of who we have and what we need to do?' In 2005 we went through a key change, as Sandy handed over responsibility for HTB to Nicky. This gave us the opportunity to re-examine and re-align our structures to support Nicky's leadership. The church cannot afford to have a static organisation.

I have been asked a few times to help other churches review their own structures, and have included three organisational review documents in the appendices of this booklet. All three are urban churches, but the principles can be applied in any context.

A particular challenge in restructuring lies in knowing when it is right to take the risk of moving on from working strictly with volunteers to having a full-time member of staff. This is an enormous step. At HTB the Alpha course had grown to 120 people before we took on paid staff to support it.

Pray into the vision

Everything we do is based upon prayer. We pray that the activities we do are consistent with the vision that God has in mind for us. We pray that God will refine our vision, and will help us to discern it. We pray constantly, and sometimes we find we are in a position where that is all that we can do. Without prayer the vision will never flourish.

[1] A pastorate is a smaller grouping in the church where people meet to grow as Christians. For further information, see Pastorates – Life at the Heart of the Church (Alpha International, 2003, forthcoming edition 2006).

Building the team

We have always relied on volunteer support from the congregation to enable every ministry in the church to operate effectively. This voluntary support continues today, even though we have more staff than many churches.

Most people are longing to be involved. Their participation enables them to assume ownership of the church's ministries.

From the children's work to the worship team, to the Alpha course at HTB itself, we enjoy the dedication and commitment of our congregation. In many ways the staff sees its role as enabling the participation of the congregation in God's vision for the church.

As the body of Christ, every member of every church congregation has a part to play in the fulfilment of that church's vision. Most people are longing to be involved. Their participation enables them to assume ownership of the church's ministries. With the participation of the whole congregation, a church can afford a big vision. Nicky spends a lot of time suggesting ways each person can play a part, and every job is significant - even if it seems minor from a secular point of view. He encourages everyone to express what is their passion, and he wants to release them and support them in pursuing it. For example, Nicky asked a long-standing member of the congregation what her passion was, and she said 'reducing the burden of debt.' Nicky encouraged her to establish a debt counselling service for the church which has now been launched.

Recruitment is of the highest priority. If you get the right people they will transform what you are trying to do. Similarly, recruiting the wrong people, whether as staff or volunteers, can create real obstacles.

Once the wrong person has been appointed it is often harder to put things right. It is certainly more difficult than leaving a position open, and then patiently waiting for the right person to come along.

People, not technology, make the difference. Tools and products can be seductive because they make life easier, but ultimately it will be the right person who drives a ministry – not equipment or resources. We have found that investing in getting and keeping the right people always pays off.

However, actually getting people involved is not always straightforward. Over the years we have identified effective approaches for getting this done.

Identify the jobs that need to be done

Once you have established your vision and your plan for the coming year, start by listing all the jobs that will need to be done, either by staff or volunteers. List everything, from opening up the church on a Sunday morning, organising the church accounts and arranging the flowers, right through to leading Alpha groups and running the children's work.

You might find at some point you have a particular ministry – perhaps children's work or Alpha – that becomes too unwieldy to be co-ordinated by a part-time or even spare-time volunteer. At this stage you might consider employing people – not necessarily to do all the work themselves, but to co-ordinate the volunteer activity more effectively.

Place value on management and administration

Good administration is absolutely key to the realisation of your vision. I was once chatting to a curate running Alpha. They were running a morning and evening Alpha course. The evening course had over a hundred guests, and I asked what sort of structure they had to help with a programme of that size. That church did not allow any of the clergy to have administrative support. To me it seemed crazy that a pastor's time should be taken up doing all the administration behind a large Alpha course.

> We look for people that are 'can-do' people; who say things like 'Leave that with me'.

It is essential to get good administrative support and back-up behind what you are doing. You might be able to do mailing and handouts yourself, but perhaps that time would be better spent preparing a talk or doing pre-marriage counselling. That would especially apply if there is someone in your church with administrative gifts, longing to play a part in the vision of your church.

We have needed to learn to identify people with administrative gifts. These are not necessarily people that have a great deal of secretarial experience, but they have the attitude and skills of an administrator. We look for people that are 'can-do' people; who say things like 'Leave that with me' and get the job done without fuss; who simplify rather than complicate processes, and leave everyone clear about their responsibilities. Having the right administrator can transform your working life, and it is important that leadership committees ensure that the clergy are properly supported in this way.

In the early days of Alpha I had a Personal Assistant, Bonnie, who revolutionised my working life. She asked me, 'What is your biggest frustration?' I told her that what frustrated me most was that I tended to be in meetings from 9am until 6.30pm, and never seemed to have enough time to put into effect what I was supposed to be doing. You will all know what that feels like. I could not concentrate on meetings because I knew my work was piling up – and so were all the action points from previous meetings.

Bonnie just replied, 'Well, not to worry, I'll come in early every morning and we'll 'offload' all of the action points from the day before. Then I can get started with the work.' I was then free to do everything else I should have been doing.

That sounds simple, but it's really only simple to someone with that particular gift. To have the right person, who understood my way of working and wanted to support me, made all the difference.

Clearly define the roles

Whether you are working with volunteers or employing paid staff, it is essential that the expectations concerning the role – from both sides – are clearly expressed, and mutually understood, before you appoint someone.

Before a person agrees to take on a role in the church, give them this sort of breakdown (job brief):
- *An idea of the overall vision of the church and the project they will be involved with, and how their role fits into it. Full commitment is essential.*
- *The general objectives of the role and its specific responsibilities.*
- *A job brief (whether volunteer or paid staff), including:*
  Specific timing of meetings they will be required to attend.
  The frequency of meetings.
  Other commitments that come with the role.
  An explanation of how much preparation time you believe this role

would take.
An understanding *of how long you would like the role to last.*
For example, Alpha leaders commit for thirteen weeks, to cover
the course, the training, the Weekend, and the Celebration Supper.
The name of the person *to whom will they be responsible.*
It is also helpful to identify those they should approach for
guidance and support.
The extent of their responsibility*, and the boundaries within which*
they will work.
Clarity *on what expenses will be reimbursed.*

This process is essential to avoid misunderstandings. *See Appendix 2*
for an example of a job brief.

Advertise the need

It is important that your congregation knows the volunteer needs
of the church. Once you have identified your list, promote the
options to the congregation. You can use notices in the service and
announcements in the Sunday service sheet to promote a particular
or urgent need.

However, for key roles, and particularly leadership roles such as
pastorate leaders or Alpha leaders, we do not advertise the need.
Often in this situation a more personal approach can yield
better results.

Hand pick the right people for the right jobs – particularly the key roles

It is important to take a proactive approach to building your team,
rather than simply waiting for them to come to you. A key skill required
for those in church leadership, at any level, lies in identifying those in
the congregation who can help – and asking them for that help.

When we know what people's gifts are, we can then match them to a particular role. When we ask for help, people know that we have confidence in their ability to perform the functions. The very act of being asked is an encouragement to them.

Furthermore you should be looking all the time for gifted people who can make a contribution to the vision, even though you may not have a specific role for them yet.

It is important to take a proactive approach to building your team, rather than simply waiting for them to come to you.

Here are four areas to consider:

Skill
When recruiting, be aware of your own weaknesses. Get people involved who are better than you in the area concerned. You must get people whose skills complement your own, and supplement your weaknesses. It is hard to acknowledge our own weaknesses. The danger is that many of us have a tendency to recruit people like ourselves because we are then not threatened by them. This process can be unconscious. A much more fruitful solution is to consciously recruit people who shine in areas in which you do not – it is a strength to acknowledge that you cannot do everything.

Look out for gifts in each member of the congregation. Encourage people to identify and develop them, and invite them to participate in the activities for which you think they have a leaning. For example, encourage those with gifts of leadership to train for pastorate leadership, and urge the artistic to take responsibility for the aesthetic expression of the church. Inspire people with musical talents to develop skills in worship, and ask technical experts to provide IT support for the church. People appreciate being picked out and chosen for a role. Invite them to take part rather than passively waiting for them to ask to be involved. This is what I mean:

Jamie McLean was in our congregation and absolutely loved the vision of Alpha. She just turned up one day and said, 'I want to help.' To begin with she had the mundane job of database entry (we had so many people calling about Alpha that we needed to build a database), and for days Jamie ploughed on doing just that.

It was only when somebody asked me if I knew about her background that I bothered to find out. I discovered that Jamie had been a management consultant for an international firm, and had been responsible for installing complex computer systems for multinational companies. She had an MBA from one of the best business schools in the world – and there she was at HTB punching data into the computer.

The moment I found out, I knew she was someone we had to move to another role. There wasn't a specific job for her, but she and I worked together to carve out a remit that suited her skills. In fact Jamie went on to become my right hand person in those early days of the explosion of Alpha, because she had all the skills I did not have. She designed and put in place the entire infrastructure that we would need in the church to be prepared for the growth of Alpha. I knew what we needed to do but I did not know how to do it. Jamie was absolutely the right person for the task.

Relationship

Good inter-staff relations are so important. We have worked hard to establish strong working relationships and friendships within the staff team, and particularly within the leadership. Friendship within the leadership team of the church has proved to be a driving force in the vision of HTB. It was essential for me to like and get on with Jamie for her to function well as my right hand person. We enjoyed spending time together and working together, and it made the job that much more enjoyable and satisfying. Nicky has a strategy group around him, and it is important that he gets on well with them and enjoys spending time with them, as this is a key group who meet three hours per week to implement the vision. Visitors to HTB have remarked on the level of real and meaningful friendship amongst the staff and volunteers.

Organisational fit

A central lesson for us has been to make sure that the people we have brought into the heart of the organisation have shared the values and culture we have sought to establish within the church. Will they represent you well? Will they answer the phone appropriately? Will they handle conflict with grace?

Humility

In our experience, those people who offer their gifts humbly are those who are really ready and willing to serve. We have learned to be wary of those who put themselves forward too enthusiastically because they might have their own agenda in mind, and might not be properly focused on the vision. Christian character is the primary qualification for leadership roles.

Brief thoroughly

Once people accept roles, whether as staff members or volunteers, it is vital that they are then given further information before they start. Once they have had time to review the job brief (discussed earlier), we schedule a meeting to:

- *Review the parameters of the role*
- *Introduce them properly to the person they will be responsible to*
- *Meet other people working on the project so that they get the whole picture, and understand where their roles fit in with others.*

When we run an event at HTB many members of the congregation are involved in a whole range of activities, from meeting and entertaining guests, to welcoming people as they arrive. There are also co-ordinating roles, like heading up the team serving tea and coffee, and overseeing the stewards. Each role has its own job brief, and we talk it through with those people so that they understand what their job is, what they need to do, and when.

Though we choose leadership positions carefully, we allow leaders to choose their own teams, so that they take responsibility for the people around them. We tell them: 'Build up your own team. You select the people who are going to do the work.' And so we grant ownership and responsibility within the parameters of roles.

Avoid burn out – spread the load

In most church communities 20 per cent of the congregation do 80 per cent of the work. This is true of many organisations. Identifying this 20 per cent is a key challenge for any leader.

In most church communities 20 per cent of the congregation do 80 per cent of the work.

Once someone is identified as a keen volunteer or staff member and proves to be a valuable asset to the church team, beware of falling into the over-use trap. Remember that people get burn out. It is so important that when you find somebody exceptionally good, you do not overburden them by increasingly eating into their time, energy and commitment. Spread the load and give others the chance to get involved.

It is crucial for church leaders to be aware of their own potential to burn out. The importance of delegation, where appropriate, cannot be over-emphasised.

At one stage in the growth of Alpha and HTB I was heavily burdened with an awful lot of responsibility. It seemed everybody just kept off-loading work onto me.

Staff would come in on a Friday afternoon with a 'major problem' to solve. In those days my response was:'Don't worry. Leave it with me and I'll have a look at it.'

So on Friday night I would take home two briefcases of work. I would struggle all weekend trying to solve problems, while the person concerned had a relaxing weekend.

An article a friend sent me from the Harvard Business Review[2] altered all that. The article highlighted the issue of the burdens of employees falling squarely onto the manager's back. I felt it absolutely applied to my current situation. Upon reading it, my strategy changed. Now my response is entirely different. I now reply: 'Well, that is a problem. I'll tell you what, I promise to meet you first thing Monday morning. You go away this weekend and come back with three proposals that might solve it.'

...give space for people to take the initiative and the risk...

This change in approach has made an enormous difference to the way both I and my team work. Not only has it taken some of the pressure off me, it has reduced the bottleneck that I used to create. This has allowed my team greater responsibility and ownership of their projects, while still enjoying the security of my supervision. Of course the tough part of the process is allowing people to sometimes make mistakes. But as a leader it is imperative that you give space for people to take the initiative and the risk, or you will stifle all that they have to offer.

Acknowledge when things aren't working out

Despite any amount of planning or briefing, there will always be times when projects or people simply fail to work. It is inevitable, and it is also inevitable that these situations will be painful. Failure to confront such problems when they occur will benefit neither the individual nor the organisation.

You must face these situations by talking promptly and clearly to the person concerned. In my experience, as long as these issues are resolved with candour and love, people will respond. They appreciate honest feedback. In the end you will also have to communicate with those who have witnessed the problem or been affected by its consequences. I have found this one of the most challenging areas of my role, but keeping the vision in mind has helped me to succeed in these necessary conversations.

Give thanks regularly and appropriately

Make sure you take the time to thank your volunteers carefully, regularly and appropriately. They are the life-blood of the church. The contribution they make must be recognised and affirmed. At HTB we hold a party, usually at Christmas, for all the volunteers who contribute to the life of the church. We thank them for participating.

We always ensure that at the end of each term those who have helped with the Alpha course, the Marriage course, the children's work and so on are properly thanked. This is done both verbally (and can be as simple as just saying thank you on an individual basis), and by personal letter. We also make a small gift to those who have taken on the job of leadership, or have shown exceptional commitment.

[2] William Onken Jr. and Donald L. Wass, 'Who's Got the Monkey?', (Harvard Business Review, November – December 1974)

Working together

When you know and understand your vision, and have identified the key people to help you realise it, you must agree on a plan of action.

How will decisions be made and communicated? How will decisions then be put into effect and followed-up? Once issues have been decided, all those involved must know and follow the agreed steps. This will require dedicated commitment on your part. The result will be great satisfaction, as you and your team start to achieve your objectives with efficiency and few misunderstandings.

What, when and to whom

When I first arrived at HTB, few routine processes were in place. I set about considering how I could give people the authority to make decisions at the appropriate level. I knew that if I got it right, I would be free to consider the broader strategic issues, and work on those things within my own area of expertise. We looked closely at all concerned. What meetings did they attend? To whom did they report daily? As mentioned in 'Building the team', it is essential for all involved to know their specific responsibilities, so that they can get on with the job. They also need to understand how they fit into the big picture. Without this knowledge they will not get answers to issues outside their areas of direct responsibility.

While we encourage people to communicate directly as much as possible, we have found that a routine schedule of meetings gives people the consistent opportunity to talk things through and make decisions. We have a number of different meetings at HTB. First of all, we have the PCC, which is our elected body of church leaders. You probably have a similar thing. It may or may not be functioning as you would like.

Sandy shared at many conferences how he worked to raise the sights of the PCC, and redefine how it worked. He spoke about how challenging it was to transform that body from a group concerned with such things as redecorating the lavatories, to one which could discuss weightier matters of vision. Nicky continues to keep the PCC focused on the key issues facing the church, and they are always consulted when there is an issue that has major financial implications or represents a major change in the vision. Every time it meets, the PCC is updated on all important aspects of the church. The day-to-day running of the church is delegated to a senior group of staff members who meet weekly.

When we were a smaller church, it was easier to make sure everybody understood the vision – where we were all going and the part we all played. It was easier to ensure the values were disseminated to the groups working to pull it all together. As we have grown, we have had to implement a departmental or team structure, so that information can be communicated and discussed with smaller groups.

Each department or area of church life is encouraged to have a weekly team meeting, to encourage the departments to communicate about their different projects. Particular projects will also have specific meetings with people from different departments. Once the vision and strategy have been agreed, the projects can be managed without intervention so long as staff know the boundaries.

How

We must make the best use of everyone's time. People often make the mistake of calling a meeting for the sake of it. The purpose of a meeting is to make and implement decisions, generate ideas, reach a consensus of opinion, or move a project or an idea forward to the next stage.

An effective meeting requires some basic work beforehand. Check that the necessary people can attend. Send out an agenda in advance with the relevant documents. This will enable people to know what to expect, and will help them prepare. Ask the relevant people to speak on items that are their responsibility.

At the actual meeting, make sure that an action plan is established. Everyone should leave knowing which actions are their responsibility and when they are expected to have completed them.

You must establish the date of the next meeting. Get the minutes out immediately so that everybody knows exactly what is expected, and remember to bring your diary to every meeting so you can plan the next one.

At HTB, meetings are an essential function for organising events and projects. It therefore goes without saying that the right people must be present and that meetings are run effectively, with carefully planned agendas and accurate minutes and action points. These action points should be reviewed at the beginning of the next meeting.

I remember being at two meetings where I noticed nobody was taking any minutes; I should have picked up on it on both occasions. When topics become complicated and there are no minutes to fall back on, you can easily forget what was agreed and who was supposed to be doing what.

From the very beginning, I always documented everything that I needed to act upon in my 'Red Book' – an A4 hardbound book of lined paper. In any meeting, if I have to implement a proposed action on anything, or if anything needs to be done, I always log it as we go along. I have a good memory and juggle lots of things, but no one can remember everything that is agreed in a meeting.

Gradually we introduced the habit of all attendees bringing a notebook and diary to each meeting. We could then note key actions and decisions and agree times for future meetings or events then and there.

While our meetings continue to become more productive, it is an ongoing discipline to remind people of what makes an effective meeting.

My personal strategy at a meeting is to state its purpose, or ask the person in the chair to state it for all. Everybody attends a meeting with personal expectations or understanding, so it is refreshing when the purpose of the meeting is made plain for everyone. Then you can continually return to that stated purpose and stay on track.

John Valentine was a curate at HTB. He later started a new church plant in London. When I asked him about his experience of working at HTB, this is what he said:

> One of the things that struck me most on coming to HTB was both the strategic and fruitful way in which meetings were used. There is also something of a vision-generating and vision-perpetuating feel to them. Meetings never just happen for the sake of having a meeting.

Other meetings

Once a week we have a senior staff meeting. This is not an administration meeting. This is a vision and a prayer and a bigger picture meeting. We make time to have lunch together. If anyone is worried about something, this gives us an opportunity to pray and talk about it. This meeting is not concerned with the detail of things, but rather with the bigger picture of what is happening, and what we should be looking at and doing.

We are a community first and foremost. We have prayer meetings for all the full-time staff once a week. For that meeting we discourage absence. Of course if we are on annual leave that is different, but generally we like all the staff to be together on that day. We are a community first and foremost, and we have to come together once a week to support and encourage one another. We have almost an hour together and we worship, we have a talk and then we pray about what is going to happen in the next week. We also have feedback from the past week, which is important because everybody then feels involved.

We really appreciate when people share stories at this meeting of how God is changing people's lives, especially if we have been stuck behind a desk all week.

The people doing a lot of work behind the scenes are as involved as those doing the upfront ministry. Tuesday is almost like a Sunday service for the staff.

A note on pastoral care and meetings

When I first arrived at HTB I would often see members of staff praying for one another in meetings. Of course it is vital for all of us to be regularly prayed for and to receive all that God has for us. But what would start off as a meeting about how to plan Parish Day would often turn into something altogether different and this was frustrating our progress. We have now established a clear distinction between our pastoral and administration time. If a pastoral issue emerges we will arrange another time to meet and pray about it.

We also make sure there are plenty of opportunities for personal prayer – either in pastorates, staff meetings or prayer meetings.

Alpha continues to be one of the most anointed ministries of our times. Optimizing the full redemptive potential of Alpha in local churches is something Tricia Neill knows better than anyone in the world. This book will support the work of the local church.
BILL HYBELS, SENIOR PASTOR, WILLOW CREEK COMMUNITY CHURCH, CHICAGO

Tricia Neill is one of the most effective managers that I have come across. Her focus on the practical and actionable is intense, and results in a lot more getting done than is the norm. I'd highly recommend any manager to read this short but tremendously helpful booklet.
ALISTAIR M. HANNA, FORMER SENIOR PARTNER, MCKINSEY AND COMPANY

Holy Trinity Brompton and Alpha are both phenomenally successful organisations, and this booklet gives you an insider's view of the principles that led to their growth. Tricia Neill shares these principles without any trace of pride, and with a simplicity and honesty that is endearing. I recommend this book to those who want tried and tested principles to help their churches grow.
PASTOR AGU IRUKWU, SENIOR PASTOR, JESUS HOUSE, LONDON

Drawing on her years of experience in both the corporate world and a thriving church community, Tricia Neill has given us a template for turning vision into action. Like the Alpha course, it too will prove to be a valuable tool for those desiring to lead their churches into the future.
PHIL JEANSONNE, SENIOR PASTOR, THE VINEYARD CHURCH, NEW ORLEANS

From Vision to Action is more than simply another 'how to' church growth booklet. It is a consultation with one of the clearest and most encouraging strategic thinkers in the Christian movement today.
DR TORY BAUCUM, ASSOCIATE PROFESSOR OF PREACHING AND CHURCH RENEWAL, ASBURY THEOLOGICAL SEMINARY

This is a fast-moving and clearly written booklet that every church leader should read. Tricia demonstrates how she has helped take a vision and played a huge part in building something that will last.
MARK BAILEY, LEAD PASTOR, TRINITY CHELTENHAM & NEW WINE LEADERSHIP TEAM

From Vision to Action is easy to read, practical, and realistic, and shows an understanding based on hands-on experience of how to move a church forward into God's vision, and how to keep it there.
CHARLES WHITEHEAD, CATHOLIC EVANGELISATION SERVICES

Tricia Neill is wonderfully practical in all she sets her mind to, and not least the details of making church happen in practice. This is a treasure chest of Godly insights that I have found profoundly helpful - not just as I read it, but also as I put it into practice. **REVD RIC THORPE, ST PAUL'S CHURCH SHADWELL, LONDON**

Tricia Neill is the real thing. She has a spectacular spiritual gift of administration. My experience has been that she subdues chaos and releases life. This book shows how the body of Christ struggles to flourish without proper administration. The wisdom distilled here in generous and easy to read fashion will strengthen and liberate the church to be more truly itself. SIMON DOWNHAM, SENIOR VICAR, ST PAULS HAMMERSMITH, LONDON

This booklet is a recipe for success in the local church. Use it and you experience the change. GRAEME PARIS, EXECUTIVE DIRECTOR, WILLOW CREEK ASSOCIATION UK

This vitally important publication can lead Christian groups and churches from a hand to mouth existence to one of purpose and passion. GERALD COATES, PIONEER, SPEAKER, AUTHOR, BROADCASTER

From Vision to Action draws out the real workings and 'goings-on' behind the scenes, and allows other churches to learn from what God has taught HTB over the last few years. FROG AND AMY ORR-EWING, ALL SAINTS CHURCH, PECKHAM, LONDON

HTB is a church with a passionate concern for God's glory, a genuine concern for the Church at large, a faithfulness to prayer, and a spirit of humility with a childlike dependence on the work of the Spirit and His grace. With these values in place, it is not a wonder that leadership and management principles work so effectively. There is something special happening here. It needs to be reflected on for the benefit of others. I am glad From Vision to Action does that. REVD TERRY WONG, ST JAMES' CHURCH, HONG KONG

Tricia Neill has written a superb booklet that should give a huge amount of help to any harried church minister or overwhelmed church administrator. I wish I had had such a book many years ago, to help me through the daunting task of moving a church forward. MALCOLM ROUND, RECTOR, ST MUNGO'S BALERNO

This booklet is filled with nuggets of practical wisdom for local churches about how to turn God-given vision into reality. Tricia shares the effective strategies and managements that have enabled the life-changing ministries of Alpha and HTB to 'take off' all over the world. REVD LYNDON BOWRING, CHAIRMAN, CARE

Effective ministry should be the goal of every Christian and their church. Drawing upon her experience at Holy Trinity Brompton, Tricia Neill contributes valuable insights to encourage this. ARCHDEACON DR RAYMOND MULLER, NATIONAL DIRECTOR, ALPHA NEW ZEALAND

This will become a core point of reference for the leadership of our church. REVD JOHN VALENTINE, PRIEST-IN-CHARGE, ST GEORGE'S CHURCH HOLBORN, LONDON

Managing new initiatives

New initiatives always arise out of a growing vision, and managing them well is essential to ensuring that the work you undertake is carried out efficiently and effectively. All large-scale projects will always be presented to the PCC for approval before we undertake them.

As we have grown, we have had to implement new systems and facilities. In my time at HTB we have instigated several major projects. One of our most important and difficult projects was to create a single database of congregation names and addresses. Other initiatives we have undertaken include projects as diverse as putting a first floor into our church hall, creating Alpha and HTB websites, and creating evangelistic Christmas carol services. We have also conducted telephone training for all staff, extended the office space in our sister church, and created a single, automated diary of all church activities. The list is endless and each project seems to require a different set of skills.

When we start a new project, large or small, we have found it essential to have someone on the team who has a good, basic understanding of project management and its principles, as well as personal experience of managing. With project management an awful lot of common sense is involved – although on larger projects we do involve professional architects and IT people. For smaller projects, our minimum checklist typically looks like this:

- *Project Goal or Objective or Product*
- *Plan*
  Start date
  Tasks

    * *Start and end dates for each*
    * *Defining personal responsibility*
    * *The expected result of the task*
  End date
  • *Estimated cost.*

We also establish a schedule of project meetings to review progress. We evaluate the actual activities going on and compare them with the project plan. Are we on target? Are we behind in some ways? Changes in schedule or budget need to be reviewed with the appropriate leaders – for example, the church council. Each project needs time devoted to communicating its purpose to the congregation and for training. There must also be a plan for the continuing operation and maintenance of the completed project.

Each new initiative should be effectively managed. If not, people will be hesitant to take on new ones. Good project management means resources and enthusiasm are not dissipated. We have found that investing in project management training for staff and volunteers has paid handsome dividends.

Follow-up

For every project you undertake: Plan it. Do it once. Debrief. Write up what you have learned about how to do it. This way, when you do it again the following year, it will be improved based on the document you have pulled together. You then go through the whole process again. It is simply learning from experience.

For every project

you undertake:

Plan it.

Reviewing every project or event requires discipline. Most of us complete one project, become desperate to leave it behind, and then embark immediately on the next. But reviewing

Do it once.

Debrief.

an event or project, however successful, will be hugely beneficial for future plans.

After every event, we encourage guests to complete a feedback form so we can review how it went. We also ask people to gather stories, testimonies or general anecdotal feedback on how successful the event or project has been – what God has been doing, and the influence it might or might not have had. Some of these stories are included in the church newspaper.

We have a policy of holding a review meeting for the team directly involved in any project. A simple process you might use in a review meeting is to ask three questions:

- *What went well?*
- *What didn't go so well?*
- *What would we do differently next time?*

If you fail to go through this process, you will find yourself reinventing the wheel, and repeating mistakes over and again. This system ensures that you will keep improving. It also allows the people involved in the project to celebrate their success, as well as work through any failures and look at how it could be done better next time.

A note on technology

As many new initiatives incorporate the use of technology, I thought it would be appropriate to mention our experience of computer systems. Technology is there to help us and to speed things up. It plays a massive part in our working lives, and we have been able to communicate much more widely and swiftly because of email and the internet.

There are advantages and disadvantages. We never forget that we are in a people business, and you will never get a group to move with you if you stick to email. I never think of Nicky as being a remote leader. He recognises the importance of human interaction alongside electronic communication. He also has a policy of signing letters personally. This personal touch echoes Sandy's original vision of making all members of the HTB parish feel as embraced and valued as a guest on an Alpha course.

We only take on new technology when we think it is going to help us in what we are trying to do. We review the costs and benefits of technology carefully. We also have to be absolutely certain that we have the skills to use and maintain it.

Keeping going

I hope the techniques and ideas discussed in this booklet will help you move and enhance your vision. They have developed from years of work – and we are still working on them! If you take the time to put a few ideas into practice, you will notice a difference. I hope this will encourage you to try a few more.

Working for a church is more than a job; it is a vocation and a passion. We need the active involvement of the Spirit and the support of the church community if we are to succeed.

After many years at HTB I remain amazed at the perseverance and dedication of its leaders, staff and congregation. As we have grown and changed, our ministry has brought about fresh challenges which constantly motivate me.

Sometimes we can get so tied up with 'realising the vision' that we lose sight of what it is really all about. At such times we begin to struggle and it is then that I know I need to do three things:

I must step back and take a broader view. When you are working daily on seeing a small part of the vision being fulfilled, it is important to step out of the detail and remind yourself of where you have come from and where you are going. Review your progress and see how what you're doing ties into where you're going. I appreciate that even though I wish everything could be done yesterday, we are moving forward all the time.

I need to be sure that I stay actively at the centre of the vision.

For me at HTB this can mean choosing to help on an Alpha course and actually seeing God change lives. It also means listening to the congregation, who are growing in their ministries. I am fortunate that Nicky takes so many opportunities to address the vision anew.

Finally, and perhaps most importantly, I need to stay focused on my own journey of faith. My pastorate and personal prayer group - as well as the many opportunities to pray with fellow staff and congregation - help me enormously, and keep me focused on where I should be. Without all this, and without the ongoing work of the Spirit in my life, it would be impossible for me to fulfil this role.

Working for a church is more than a job; it is a vocation and a passion. We need the active involvement of the Spirit and the support of the church community if we are to succeed. We are a family and a community.

Tricia's top tips

While we were putting this booklet together, a few people put forward observations of what made HTB effective in pursuing its vision. They were small, practical, and sometimes seemingly insignificant ideas. I offer them here hoping that they might be of some use. In any event, I would certainly encourage you to look at your own working practices and share them with your team, so you can all work together effectively.

Have a 'Red Book'

This is one of my essential pieces of kit – basically a notebook with lined paper. Our memories can only see us so far – the Red Book does the rest.

Delegate

To successfully work towards your vision, delegation is key. Do not be tempted to think you can do it all – people are keen to help in so many different ways. Release them and release yourself to do only what you can do.

People first, then do

When you have a vision that calls for something to be done, put the people in place before you begin. Nothing gets done without the right people.

Interview well

This is very difficult so don't just rely upon yourself to interview – use others, so you have the benefit of another person's experience.

Foster teamwork and ownership

Instead of having individuals doing their own thing in isolation, enable a sense of togetherness. As far as possible, work in teams. Value every contribution. Where have we got to? What needs to be done next? What part do we play in it all?

Take risks

The turtle only advances with its head out of its shell. Be prepared to

- *Take risks*
- *Use common sense*
- *Change if it isn't right.*

Put stakes in the ground

Let me give you an example. If you are planning an event, particularly an Alpha course, announce your plan as early as possible. Put a metaphorical stake in the ground. Do this whether or not you feel fully prepared for it. Putting down these markers will keep people moving towards a goal. It allows progress to take place.

Plan, do, check, review

This tip might seem obvious but in short it is, 'Learn from experience' – which is something we do not always do.

Give feedback

I believe in honest, straightforward feedback. Do not ignore the little things because you are worried about offending somebody. If it is

done in love, and for the right motivation, feedback is always
a benefit.

Spread the message of quality

Seek excellence in everything you attempt. Always run an event or
a project to the highest possible standards. Pay great attention
to detail.

Appendix 1: organisational reviews

Church A

Church A is an Anglican church with a congregation of 700.

Organisation and Management Review

Together with the Head of HR, I spent the day with the Church Leader and the team at Church A. The purpose of the day was to see if we could assist the Church Leader with some suggested structures. This summary report details our observations and recommendations.

1. Core team / board
It is important to establish a core team around the Church Leader. All activities and ministries are to report into one of the board members.

The board would be the Church Leader, the Assistant Minister, the Curate, the Family Life and Morning Alpha Leader, the Pastoral Coordinator and the Office Manager.

2. Meeting structures
Each meeting should have clear aims and objectives, an agenda (timed or at least a time limit on the whole meeting) and be minuted.
Suggested meetings:

2.1 Vision and strategy meeting
This would include prayer and would be held once a month or once a term. Attendees would be the board members. There would be no administration at this meeting; instead it would be much more forward looking.

2.2 Core team meeting, aka board meeting
This would be once a week and would give approval for new

projects, expenditure over a certain amount and act as an escalation point for policy-making decisions. This is not a vision meeting.

2.3 Whole staff meeting
This would be once a week and should incorporate a run-through of events coming up during the week.

2.4 One-to-ones
a) The Church Leader with direct reports
These should be fortnightly. It is an opportunity for each of the core team to review their areas of responsibility with the Church Leader and to report how they are moving projects and tasks forward.
b) Core team and direct reports
These should be weekly or fortnightly. Similar to above, each manager should review areas of responsibility with people on their teams.

2.5 Services meeting
This should include the Church Leader, the Family Life and Morning Alpha Leader, the Assistant Minister, the Curate, the Pastoral Coordinator, the Children's Worker, the Youth Worker and the Worship Leader. These should be weekly. The aim is to discuss feedback and actions arising from the previous Sunday and include planning for the next Sunday services.

3. Technical requirements for the office
There is an immediate requirement for the following to be addressed:
- *Proper management of incoming telephone calls.*
- *Networking of PCs for sharing information, particularly the database.*

These areas can be discussed in more detail once the Office Manager is in place.

4. Working time for support staff

There is a need for continuity of effort in bringing together the requirements for Sundays (in particular) and possibly other events such as Alpha courses. It is therefore recommended to have support staff responsible for these events present on the day to ensure all goes to plan. Responsibility for smooth running at the event will be with support staff NOT the pastoral staff, freeing the latter to do the course teaching and look after the guests.

5. Suggested responsibilities

Church Leader
Clergy role and oversees everything but with particular 'hands on' for:
- Prayer
- General synod
- Special courses
- Accountability of core team

Assistant Minister
(reports to Church Leader)
- Clergy role
- Alpha
- Mission
- Men's ministry
- Post-Alpha discipleship course
- Pastoring
- Pastoral care support

Family Life and Morning Alpha Leader
(reports to Church Leader)
- Family life
- Children
- Morning Alpha
- Parish weekend
- Women's work

Pastoral Co-ordinator
(reports to Church Leader)
- Pastorate co-ordinator
- Home groups
- Prison Alpha
- Publishing, promotions and communications
- Registration forms
- Link to Home Focus
- Parish magazine

Office Manager
(reports to Church Leader)
- IT
- Web
- Finance
- Building project
- General administration
  and reception
- Facilities management
- Diary
- Database
- Personnel

Curate (reports to Church Leader)
- Clergy role
- Prison Alpha
- Ministry and leadership training
- Worship team
- Pastor
- Youth

- Special services
- Sunday services
- Bookshop
- Newcomers
- Volunteers

6. Challenges

a) New appointments

We think you have a wonderful core team, which is a great
blessing and a key foundation on which to build. The appointment
of the Office Manager is a key next step. Secondly, recruitment
of quality support staff is key to moving the vision forward.

b) Enlarging the Pastoral Co-ordinator's role

In section 5, we have considerably enlarged the Pastoral Co-
ordinator's areas of responsibility. They (as well as the Family Life
and Morning Alpha leader) will need further support staff to carry
the workload. At present, we have indicated Bookshop as part of
the Pastoral Co-ordinator's brief. This was because logically it fits
with publications and communications but we appreciate there

could be issues with this so this can be a discussion item.

c) Team working

Presently, people tend to work independently. There is a need to work more in teams. An example would be:

The Family Life and Morning Alpha Leader is responsible for the parish weekend. Therefore they need to gather together a project team to cover areas such as: children, youth, administration (promotion and registration and volunteer tasks) and worship. They will also need one of the clergy team to be responsible for the teaching programme at the weekend.

Another example would be the Services meeting described in 2.5

Church B

Church B is an Anglican church with a congregation of 200.

Organisational Review

Together with the Head of HR, I spent the day with the Church Leader, the Church Leader's wife and the team at Church B. The purpose of the day was to see if we could assist the Church Leader with some suggested structures. This summary report details our observations and recommendations.

The vision
To have three vibrant and dynamic churches forming the Church B District Church Council; to be community based and to have the full involvement of the local people.

In our individual meetings with the team we asked what they regard to be the key priorities. The clearest expression was summarised as Sundays, Pastorates, Alpha and Community Work. That said, not everyone in the team was clear about the priorities, and in this sense it may be beneficial for the Church Leader to articulate his vision and how the priorities fit into it at a forthcoming staff meeting.

Staff structure
We recommended that the structure be further defined, so for there to be clear reporting lines, a distinction drawn between pastoral support and line management, and greater accountability for junior staff. In addition to this organisational structure, it is of course anticipated that the Church Leader and the person responsible for Pastoral Ministry will continue pastoring the team.

Leadership team

If the above structure is set in place, the leadership team will form as the Church Leader, the Curate, the Worship Leader, the person responsible for Pastoral Ministry (ideally female, if not the Church Leader's wife), and another member of clergy. It may be beneficial for this group to meet together on a fairly regular basis – perhaps weekly to begin with to roll out the vision and strategy.

Curate

We suggested that in addition to clergy responsibilities, the Curate is encouraged to take the lead in defining and implementing the strategy for 1) Alpha and 2) evangelism and community work as defined above in the vision, partnering with the person responsible for Pastoral Ministry. Clearly the Curate will need support from the team so to implement, but this adjustment in approach is an important one for the Curate to be able to operate as a senior member of the team, and not, for example, the one shopping for groceries for Alpha on a Wednesday afternoon. We exaggerate to make the point. We believe that giving the Curate responsibility for managing two (initially three with the Children's worker) Pastoral Assistants will develop their delegation and leadership skills, and that giving responsibility for the community work will ignite their passion. The Curate does not need to be the vision bearer - that will of course come from the Church Leader - but with a team of Pastoral Assistants the Curate will be better equipped to lead. A mentor could provide valuable support for the Curate.

Need for an implementer

The Church Leader made a comment about things just happening at HTB. Having met with the team, it is evident that no one on the staff shines as a natural implementer. Someone to set the operation in motion and make it happen so to release the clergy and ministry-focused staff. I think we are all agreed that the current key high capacity volunteer (who has a consultancy/technology background) would be ideal in this role. They are passionate about the vision and able to volunteer their time. We would recommend that they sit in the core team as a consultant, taking a special projects role and reporting into the Church Leader and perhaps occasionally participating in the leadership team meetings.

Pastoral Assistants

In the short term we would recommend that the Pastoral Assistants have their roles defined with a job description, acknowledging that things need to be fluid, especially in a team of this size. Looking to the Autumn, if one Pastoral Assistant is to leave for theological training it could be that the youth worker steps into this role. This may then best fit reporting into the additional Clergy, allowing the Curate to ascertain the exact skill set required for his team - possibly verging, logistics and administration. In time, the Pastoral Assistants may be required to provide the Worship Leader and the person responsible for Pastoral Ministry with administration support - we recommend that this be assigned by the Church Leader so to maintain clear reporting lines.

Infrastructure: technology & database

The key high capacity volunteer is running with this project and appears to have an excellent grasp of the opportunities and challenges.

Church Leader's PA

As discussed, the Church Leader's PA is not attending the Sunday morning service at the church. We recommend that this is addressed. During the week the Church Leader's PA is often the face and voice for the church within the parish and it would be of great benefit if they were able to get to know the congregation so to effectively support the Church Leader and run the office. When the Church Leader is away at weekends, and if both the Church Leader and his PA are away in August, there needs to be a solution to access emails and post. Similarly, some of the team mentioned that the PA is sometimes in a vulnerable position when alone in the office and opening the door.

Succession plan
Given that the Curate has only committed to Church B for a further year until the end of his curacy, it would be helpful to plan some form of clergy succession strategy.

Communication strategy
Many of the team talked about empowering the congregation to get connected and involved, from being absorbers to transformers. Currently this is happening through the pastorates. The Curate's wife or the key high capacity volunteer would both be great at pulling together a strategy for communication with the congregation.

The Curate's wife
The Curate's wife will be a great asset to the team, and definitely worth approaching to see if she is able to spearhead something - mother and toddlers for example. People speak very highly of her and we are sure she would love to be involved.

Church C

Church C is a multi-denominational church with a congregation of 600, with a further 350 people attending weekly outreach events.

Organisational Review

Together with the Head of HR, I met with the Church Leader and his core team at Church C. The purpose of the day was to see if we could assist the Church Leader with some suggested structures. This summary report details our observations and recommendations.

The vision

Following a period of explainable disorientation, the last 18 months have seen a period of consolidation for Church C. The leadership team is new and a strategy has been established. Church C uses a group of 12 or G12 model – a fresh vision of church originating in Columbia. Part of this vision involves structuring and leading the church with two core groups of 12, who in turn have a faith goal to disciple their own 12, and equip each individual to do the same thereafter.

Strong core activity exists in 1) caring for the homeless and 2) overseas mission – reflecting on the church and the kingdom, both local and global. The vision is to position themselves to reach the thousands for Christ, rather than simply adding numbers to the membership total – 'the world is our parish' philosophy.

Recommendations:

1. Core team structure

'Put your best people on your biggest opportunities, not your biggest problems.'

It is beneficial that a high proportion of the staff also enjoy membership of the core group of 24.

1.1 Having reviewed the structures, we would like to recommend one of two options to ensure that the Church Leader is appropriately supported and released to drive the vision forward. Either:

- *bring in a Personal Assistant for the Church Leader, under the Operations Manager or as a Church Leader direct report (see diagrams a and b).*
- *divide the current remit of the Operations Manager in anticipation of the inevitable administration growth given the end of the recent consolidation phase. Bring in another experienced manager to deliver aspects of this role. The positioning of this role would need to be handled with sensitivity given the Operations Manager's current remit, valuable relationship with the Church Leader and contribution to the church's vision (see diagram c).*

1.2 In any event, it is clear that the Operations Manager role requires definition and clarification – so as to match the Operations Manager remit and skill set.

1.3 Another way of looking at this would be to split the structure into a) ministries and b) operations. Those individuals sitting in a ministry role will inevitably need to report to the Church Leader. Aside from that, we would recommend that a number two for the Church Leader (which could be the Operations Manager) would head up all of the infrastructure teams – Finance & IT, Office, General Management and Strategic Planning (see diagram d).

1.4 We discussed at length the fact that the Office Manager is overstretched and unable to operate at a level which adds most value. It is clear that an effective office administrator is required to release the Office Manager from day-to-day administrative duties.

2. Priorities

The team is currently looking to move into a new office space. Securing a new location has to be a priority and the Church Leader requires a Project Manager to co-ordinate this activity. This could be the Church Leader's number two or another church manager who has the relevant project management and implementation skills. In addition to this, we would recommend the formation of a committee of volunteers from within the congregation who have various skills and levels of time to help on a project of this magnitude.

3. Communication

It is evident that strong channels of communication exist within the core team, both within the staff and within the two senior '12s'. To further this and to aid transparent, inclusive and timely communication, the following forums are suggested:

3.1 Staff meeting – weekly. The primary aims of such a forum are to provide a fixed point in the week for corporate prayer and worship, and an opportunity to look back and forward with respect to aspects of ministry areas and business.

3.2 Senior 24 meeting – weekly. This is already in place, and given the G12 model is definitely required. We would recommend that points of action and information flow from the staff meeting to the senior 24 meeting and vice versa, to aid a consistent approach.

3.3 Vision & strategy meeting – monthly. Only required if the weekly staff and senior 24 meetings do not provide an opportunity to discuss and brainstorm the medium / long-term picture.

4. Volunteer vision – tapping into talent

We would recommend that wherever possible, graduates of the church's leadership programme are positively encouraged to get involved and serve as their gifts and skills warrant in a volunteer capacity, in addition to serving within their 12. Establishing this model from the outset will encourage the use of volunteering in this way and limit the pressure to increase staff headcount. So as to have gravitas, such a vision for volunteering needs to be preached from the top.

5. Working practices

It is evident that all members of the core staff are fully on board with the vision and thoroughly flexible with respect to working hours. Whilst extremely beneficial, this needs to be monitored to ensure that staff do not burn out.

That said, and for the reasons discussed at our meeting, we think that where staff have responsibility for a particular aspect of ministry or event (e.g. the administration of Sunday services) they ought to be contracted to work the event. This may result in changes to contractual hours for some staff and the establishment of a time off in lieu policy.

6. Recruitment

'When in doubt, don't hire – keep looking.'

We would recommend that you continue to look for an Office Administrator and think creatively about how to attract an individual with high levels of motivation and positivity who can be shaped and nurtured by the Office Manager.

7. Church C calendar of events

Having one of the core team oversee the co-ordination of the annual calendar of events would ensure that the execution of these projects can be planned more proactively and holistically co-ordinated with the ministry workers still running with the detail. The Operations Manager or the Office Manager could fill this role. It is important to set this structure in place now so as to support the inevitable growth in number and type of events going forward and to benefit from efficiency wherever possible.

Diagram A

Diagram B

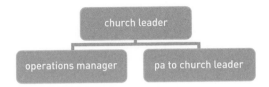

Diagram C

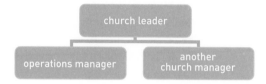

Diagram D

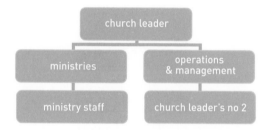

Appendix 2: job brief

Homebase Administrator

Reports to: HTB Events Manager

Role:
Homebase coordinates and facilitates ministries supporting HTB the parish church - such as Sunday services, Pastorates and HTB events. The department is responsible for supporting the clergy in all the above areas. The mission of HTB is 'the re-evangelisation of the world and the transformation of society', and the hub and starting point for this vision is HTB.

The Homebase Administrator is responsible for the following events – Classics Concerts and the Prayer Weekend. They will work with the HTB Events Project Manager on all other events as required. They will co-ordinate the publishing requirements for Homebase and also the flowers for events and Sunday services.

They will be responsible for the course administration for the New ID course and Prayer Ministry Training.

In addition, the Homebase Administrator will provide support and back up for the Clergy's executive assistant as and when required.

Liaises with:
Internally: Clergy, Publications, Communications, Maintenance, Prayer, Worship, Events Team and other departments
Externally: Some contact with outside companies and vendors required for events

Required skills:
- *Committed, enthusiastic and proactive*
- *Ability to manage multiple projects and prioritise work loads*
- *Ability to work to deadline*

- *Confidentiality*
- *Good communication skills, both verbal and written*
- *Exceptional interpersonal skills*
- *Demonstrated experience using Microsoft products such as Word, PowerPoint and Excel*
- *Events planning and events management skills.*

Job requirements and benefits:
- *Mon–Fri: Hours 9.30 am - 5.30 pm*
- *Five weeks holiday*
- *Attendance at Tuesday staff meeting 9:30 am*
- *Available to work at Christmas services, Carol services, Easter services, Annual Parish Church Meeting, Parish Day, Home Focus (the church week away) and at other events when required, for which time off in lieu will be granted.*
- *Available to work Sunday mornings or evenings when required (about once every 3 months), for which time off in lieu is granted.*

Further resources

JEREMY JENNINGS: The Church on its Knees
(Alpha International, 1998, latest edition 2001).
Drawing on his experience at Holy Trinity Brompton, Director of Prayer Jeremy Jennings has written this practical book on the development of dynamic prayer within the church.

What happens after Alpha?
Pastorates – Life at the Heart of the Church
(Alpha International, 2003, latest edition forthcoming November 2006).
Christians have always met together, and from the earliest beginnings of the church members of the community of faith have gathered in both small and large groups. This guide provides tips on how to integrate Alpha guests into the discipleship life of the church, and includes practical advice for leaders on how to set up 'pastorate' or 'mid-week' groups, including the purpose and place of pastorates, the practicalities of an evening and the role of a leader.

Integrating Alpha into the Local Church DVD
(Alpha International, latest edition forthcoming October 2006).
What sort of church are we trying to build? How do we develop a church that is relevant to today's society? In this DVD, the Rt Revd Sandy Millar discusses biblical principles for today's church and practical ways that the Alpha course can be integrated into the church.

NICKY GUMBEL: Alpha – Questions of Life
(Kingsway, 1993, latest edition 2006).
The Alpha course talks in book form. Containing the fifteen talks, this is essential reading for anyone involved in an Alpha course.

NICKY GUMBEL: How to Run the Alpha Course – Telling Others
(Kingsway, 1994, latest edition 2004).
This book imparts the vision, excitement and challenge of Alpha and is for churches who wish to run the course within their communities. It includes material from the Alpha conference and provides course administrators and leaders with insight and helpful guidance on the practicalities of Alpha.

Alpha follow-up courses

NICKY GUMBEL: **Challenging Lifestyle**
(Kingsway, 1996, latest edition 2005).
Nineteen bible studies which seek to apply Jesus' teaching on the Sermon on the Mount to our daily lives. This book shows us how Jesus' teaching flies in the face of the modern lifestyle, and presents us with a radical alternative.

NICKY GUMBEL: **Heart of Revival**
(Kingsway, 1997, latest edition 1998).
Examining ten Bible studies based on the second half of the book of Isaiah, Nicky Gumbel draws out important truths for today by interpreting what revival might mean and how we can prepare to be part of it.

NICKY GUMBEL: **A Life Worth Living**
(Kingsway, 1994, latest edition 2006).
This nine-session course, based on Paul's letter to the Philippians, is aimed specifically at those starting out in the Christian life and is ideal for those who have just completed an Alpha course. Each chapter gives practical and positive guidance on how to achieve a new and fulfilled life – a life worth living.

NICKY GUMBEL: **Searching Issues**
(Kingsway, 1994, latest edition 2004).
Nicky Gumbel tackles the seven most common objections to the Christian faith, including suffering, other religions and sex before marriage.